Happy Birthday David

A small memento

to mark a very
special coming of
age Birthday.

Audrey & David. xx.

Mildenhall
in old picture postcards

by Colin M. Dring

European Library ZALTBOMMEL/THE NETHERLANDS

GB ISBN 90 288 5751 6
© 1993 European Library – Zaltbommel/The Netherlands
Second edition, 1996.

INTRODUCTION

This book largely covers the years 1880-1930 when Mildenhall was still a quiet market town where the same families had often been running the same shops for generations. There had been a silk factory here in the 1830s and a small iron foundry but little other industry and the town was therefore badly affected by the 19th century agricultural depression. The opening of the railway in 1885 came too late to prevent a steep fall in population and the economy of the area did not begin to recover until work started on the airfield in 1931. The great Mildenhall to Australia Air Race of 1934 brought the town into the limelight for the first time in many years. RAF Mildenhall grew to become an important Bomber Command base during the Second World War and is now a large American installation, its annual air shows, the largest in the country, attracting upwards of 300,000 spectators.

The town began to expand in the 1930s but the major development came in the 1960s when an agreement was reached with the Greater London Council to transfer families here from the metropolis. New housing estates were built and a light industrial estate established to provide employment for the newcomers who have now fully integrated into local life. The history of the area, however, can be traced back to prehistoric times for excavations at High Lodge have proved that there was life here 500,000 years ago, the earliest evidence for Stone Age toolmakers in this country. This district, at the junction of the formerly marshy fenland and dry breckland, was very attractive to ancient man and there have been numerous discoveries from all archaeological periods. The Romans had a large settlement at nearby Icklingham and a ring of farmsteads around the edge of the fen. It was near one of these that the Mildenhall Treasure, a priceless hoard of Roman silver that is now in the British Museum, was found at West Row in 1943.

The manor of Mildenhall was given by Edward the Confessor to the abbot of Bury St. Edmunds and remained the property of the abbey until the dissolution of the monasteries by Henry VIII in 1536. During this time the town rose to a position of considerable importance, having an annual timber fair as well as a weekly market. Two local men, Henry de Barton and William Gregory, made their fortunes in London, both becoming Lords Mayor. It was at this time also that the magnificent parish church of St. Mary, famous for its ornately carved angel roof, was built.

The manor was later sold by the crown to the North

family, descending through several generations before passing by marriage to Sir Thomas Hanmer, a renowned Speaker of the House of Commons, and then to the Bunbury family which held it until the final sale of the last of the great estate in 1933. Many members of these families achieved fame in public life. Sir Thomas Charles Bunbury once tossed a coin with Lord Derby to decide whose name should be given to a new horse race; Derby won the toss but Bunbury's horse won the first Derby.

This is not a history of Mildenhall, although it is hoped that the captions will give some glimpses of life in the area. The content of this book has been dictated by the availability of photographs and, sadly, many roads and institutions do not appear. It is to be hoped that any interest generated by this work will bring to light many more old postcards and photographs to cover the gaps.

Acknowledgements

Firstly, I must express my gratitude to the trustees of the Mildenhall Museum for allowing use of their extensive archives and to the many individuals who have given photographs to the museum over the years. I have not attempted to acknowledge these donors personally, as in many cases copies have been received from several different sources. Mention is made in captions, where photographs have been made available from elsewhere.

Many people have given freely of their time to help me with the preparation of this book and it would be invidious to mention but a few. I must, however, express my thanks to Wilfred Bell, who first encouraged my interest in these matters and who has given so many photographs to the museum, and to Mrs. Elisabeth Brotherton, who has been so helpful over the years, whenever copies have been requested.

Finally, my work would have been much more difficult had I not had access to the bound volumes of Simpson's Directories and Monthly Magazines that were so generously bequeathed to the museum by Miss Cissie Simpson in 1991. These are mentioned later but, suffice it to say, there can be few towns the size of Mildenhall that can boast such splendid source material for the study of recent history. Mildenhall will forever be indebted to the Simpson family.

Colin M. Dring

1. Friday markets have been a feature of Mildenhall at least since 1412 when a royal charter was first obtained. The Market Cross is believed to date from the 1400s and is still nominally owned by the Lord of the Manor, although leased to the parish council since 1938 for 1 p. a year. An early Victorian drawing shows stocks still in place at the foot of the cross. Note the water pump which still stands; mains water did not come to the town until 1939. This 1896 view shows, on the far side of the High Street, the Tiger's Head, little changed, and Palmer's stationery shop, demolished in 1905.

2. The first shop to the right of the Market Cross, in 1896, was then Isaac Minns' saddlery shop. Note the fire wall, built between this shop and its neighbour. Edward Minns stripped the plaster to reveal the old oak beams in 1932. The other half of this building was then Jonathan Norman's butcher's shop, specialising in game and poultry. Later it became a cycle shop but since 1933 has been a doctors' surgery. The house on the far right, now also a doctors' surgery, was then the home of Henry Large, auctioneer and organist at the parish church for over 50 years.

3. The Cash Boot Stores returned to the Market Place in 1902, having been in exile in St. Andrew's Street since 1897. Mr. Remington, who had taken over from Garnham Bros., moved his shoe shop to the High Street in 1920 but kept this shop on as a stationer's. Behind the cross are the premises of Harry Ungless, in business as a plumber, decorator and undertaker from 1898 until his early death in 1906. His shop had been the Pettit family's bakery from the 1830s. Next on the right is a branch of Stiles where Herbert, the last of the three brothers, had his shop until he died in 1933.

4. This scene, looking up the Market Place from the High Street, dates from about 1905. Whitworth's had opened for business in 1900, with Mr. R.F. Radford as manager until the 1940s. The shop was later taken over by Adkins and then Budgens. At the top of the square is the house of Mr. R. Clarke, builder and undertaker. The façade was preserved when the office and supermarket behind were built in the 1970s. Most of the buildings in the square date to just after the disaster of 1569 when a terrible fire raged for two hours and destroyed 37 houses. (Courtesy Mrs. G. Hagan.)

5. There was a cycling club in 1882 but the sport was then too expensive to attract enough members. Another club was started in 1894 with Dr. William Dunn, a local G.P., as President and Mr. F. Peachey as Secretary. This group must be from the early days as there is an empty space where Whitworth's stores appeared in 1900. The club was reformed as The Wheelers' Cycle Club in 1932, with Mr. A.W. Neve as President and Mr. J. Mothersole as Secretary. It has since gone from strength to strength, the club's annual Dairytime Gala now being one of the most important cycling events in the country.

6. The history of the town is punctuated by numerous fires. This one occurred in September 1897, starting at the rear of Firth Bros.' grocery shop and Mr. Morley's furniture warehouse on the south side of the Market Place. The volunteer fire brigade managed to stop the blaze spreading to the home of the Misses Aldrich to the east and Mrs. Towler's pork butcher's shop to the west. The souvenir photograph lists the names of all associated with the fire brigade. A full account of the event appeared in the Mildenhall Monthly Journal, another of Simpson's efforts, in October 1897.

7. The T.S.B. corner is seen here in 1909. The present beamed appearance dates to the renovations of 1932. The first bank to trade from here was Gurney's and Co. from the early 1870s. This firm merged, largely through family connections, to become Barclay's in 1907. The national banks agreed to reduce the number of branches in use during the Second World War and this building was in use as government offices for the issue of ration books, etc. Then, in 1947, Barclay's was sold to the T.S.B. which has been here ever since. Mildenhall Museum occupied the upper floor and one room downstairs until the bank expanded in 1983.

HIGH STREET, MILDENHALL.

8. This photograph of the High Street is one of a series taken by Mr. Stanton in 1896 and published by Simpson in his History of Mildenhall. On the left are the old White Hart, Andrews' ironmongery shop and the Bell Hotel. At the very end of the street, to the left of the now Lloyds Bank, then still a private house, is a glimpse of Mab's Hall. John Wing died here, aged 101, in 1903 but in the early 1700s it had been the home of Mr. Bradbury. Squire Coe often used to meet Mr. Bradbury and Sir Thomas Hanmer in the Cock Inn where they drank and played cards late into the night, matters of which Coe always repented in his journal (published in 1994 by the Suffolk Records Society) the next day.

9. The old White Hart, seen here in the 1880s, was one of the oldest buildings in the town but, sadly, burnt down in 1910. It was run by Mr. J. Fortescue from the 1870s until 1889, when he handed over to William Willson. The off-licence to the left was later for many years Mrs. Judkins' shop but is now again part of the hotel. The ironmonger's to the right was opened by Mr. F.C. Andrews from Bury in 1882. He sold to Mr. E.J. Mutton, who also had a smithy in St. Andrew's Street, in 1893. Later the shop fell empty until reopened by Bussens and Parkin from Downham Market in 1928. This building too was destroyed by fire in 1968. (Courtesy Mr. L. Reeve.)

10. The Bell Hotel was decorated as usual for the 1909 flower show. The hotel first appeared on this site in the 1790s and rapidly took away trade from the Cock Inn opposite. Back in 1737 the Bell site, and the whole block from the White Hart back and across to St. Andrew's Street, was owned by a timber merchant who went bankrupt. The site was bought by a Mrs. Mallabar who sold in 1785 to Jane Sparhawke whose children started the Bell Hotel and also built the shop to the left. There were legal tangles when this shop was later sold off separately and the Bell and the shop each ended up with the right to occupy half of a numbered pew in the parish church.

11. Harry Parish reopened the long-established butcher's shop on the corner of the High Street and St. Andrew's Street, in 1924. It remained a butcher's in the hands of Joe Fuller, Russell Spooner, William Spooner and Mr. Golding, until Barclay's Bank returned to the town in the early 1970s. The shop to the left, now also part of Barclay's, was a chemist's shop. Mr. Chifney was here from 1853 until 1890 and then his widow to 1903. The shop then passed through the hands of Mr. Ecclestone, Mr. Forster and Mr. Gregory until the business was moved to the new shopping precinct in the early 1970s.

12. This shows the High Street soon after Harry Parish had taken over the butcher's shop in 1924. Note the carcasses displayed with scant regard for hygiene. Note also the change in the roof line after the first shop on the left, Morley's the jeweller's and watchmaker's. From here to the churchyard, round to include the old cottages in the churchyard and back to include No. 4 Mill Street, stood the old Cock Inn, a large rambling coaching inn that closed by 1821, a victim of the Bell's success. The property was bought by Arthur Gedge, a local surgeon, who made a quick profit by selling off lots which became the shops of today.

13. There was a carefree disregard for the rules of the road in this earlier view but traffic was not then a problem. This was just as well for the streets were still unsurfaced and dust was a major problem in summer. Local traders clubbed together in 1900 to buy a watering cart for £45,25 and then paid Parker Bros. £1,50 a week to water the streets. On the left, after Morley's, is Stiles' outfitters and drapers which continued here until 1933, Morley's then expanding into the premises to form a small department store. Just before the churchyard, is Mr. W. Williams' grocer's shop, to be continued by his son Maurice until the 1970s.

14. A marathon race started from the High Street in 1909 as part of the July flower show festivities, the highlight of Mildenhall's year. Shows were held annually from 1873 in the grounds of the old manor house. The weather was so bad in 1875 that the show was repeated the next day. In 1905 the show moved to Mrs. Marshall's meadow but this was never as popular and the shows petered out in 1912. They were resurrected in 1924 on Sheldrick's meadow in West Street and ran, later on Turner's meadow, until the 1940s. Special excursion trains were laid on to bring visitors to the town on show days.

15. The High Street was decorated for the second flower show of 1874 and later the rest of the town centre joined in with ever more elaborate displays. A special committee, for long run by Mr. Fortescue of the White Hart, raised funds to pay for the decorations. This 1910 example typifies the incredible amount of effort that was expended for just one day. The good luck sign to the right of Stiles' shop covers the entrance to the old Cock Inn yard. The Long Room of the Cock extended over this archway and was the scene of many of Squire Coe's misdemeanors. The next shop on the right was also part of the Stiles' complex.

16. This very early photograph of Morley's corner shows the shop still with a thatched roof. The sign above the doorway reads, MAY THE PLOUGH AND THE SPADE BE UNITED WITH TRADE. The Horticultural Society had planned annual ploughing matches to coincide with the flower shows but these attracted little interest and only two were held. The second ploughing match took place in 1874, the year that the High Street was first decorated, so it is possible that this was the occasion for this photograph to be taken although the Morley family believe that it may be as old as 1865.

17. The annual Sunday School treats were always much appreciated by local children. A procession of decorated carts took the party to the field chosen for the day's sports and picnic tea. This 1910 scene shows one of the carts from St. Peter's Sunday School on its way from West Row to Barton Mills. Note that Morley's now has a simple tiled roof. Morley's was then a watchmaker's as well as a jeweller's and later became a mini-department store. The other shops, Stiles' and Williams', have very plain fronts. The dusty state of the roadway is very evident.

18. A butcher's shop stood at the corner of St. Andrew's Street from at least 1711 until the early 1970s. Records show that John Shafton, a butcher, died here in 1711. He and two of his children were buried in the same month that year, victims of the smallpox epidemic that killed 55 people in Mildenhall. This was often called Randall's corner for Thomas Randall was in business here from 1851, being succeeded by his son Harry until 1901. It was then Burton's until Harry Parish took over in 1924. Note the interesting detail, still to be seen, on the brickwork at the corner.

19. The opposite corner of St. Andrew's Street with the High Street could well be called Lack's corner for Mr. R.A. Lack first opened his sweet shop and tobacconist's here in 1928 and the business was continued by his widow until 1979. Many still remember Mrs. Lack walking to work, pushing her invalid dog in a pram. Mr. Ernie Bond had a shop here before Mr. Lack but the site had previously been one of the town's numerous bakeries and, from the 1870s, had been managed by the Bangs family as the Junction House Bakery.

20. This is an early view of St. Andrew's Street, looking east from the High Street. The blacksmith's shop and cottages on the left were demolished in 1971 to make way for an extension to the Bell Hotel but all the buildings on the right, with the exception of the town hall, remain. This street was once called Chalk Lane and later Cock Inn Lane, but, after the old coaching inn closed, was renamed St. Andrew's Street as it led towards the parish church of that name. In 1895, it was found that the church was originally dedicated to St. Mary. The name of the church has been changed but not that of the street.

21. The town hall was built in St. Andrew's Street in 1886 at the instigation of a Mr. E. Compton who put up the capital on the condition that a consortium of local tradesmen would guarantee him a 5% return. 50p shares in a Town Hall Company were issued in 1910 but no dividend was ever paid. Reading and coffee rooms were provided here as well as a large hall. The building was sold in 1986, its centenary year, and has since been demolished to await redevelopment. Mildenhall Museum first opened here, in the former caretaker's flat, soon after the town's 1951 Festival of Britain celebrations.

22. Almost all of the town's major events were based on the town hall for nearly a century. This was the Conservative Association's dinner in 1910; 180 members were present with Sir Henry Bunbury in the chair. The hall also served as the town's first and only cinema from 1918 until the Comet opened in North Terrace in 1935. Many clubs and societies made use of the facilities, not least the Mutual Improvement Society, founded in 1872, and the Literary Institute, founded in 1851, that merged in 1881 with other groups to become the Mildenhall Institute, surviving as such until 1910.

23. This view of Mill Street from the High Street corner is from the early 1900s. The double-fronted building on the left was Mildenhall's first proper bank, opened by Oakes Bevan & Co. in about 1885, business having earlier been conducted by Isaacson's, solicitors in Mill Street. Next on the left is Potter's Wine & Spirits shop, sold to Mothersole in 1910 and later merged into the International Stores' premises. On the right is the corner of Morley's shop, followed by Felix Brown the tailor at No. 4 and Charles Stebbing's shoe shop at No. 6. Beyond is Simpson's printing shop at No. 8.

24. W.G. Mothersole's delivery lorry is seen here outside the Lamb public house, now Lamb Court, in Barton Mills in about 1920. Jack Crick is either the driver or the passenger. Mothersole was already trading from St. Andrew's Street when he bought Potter's Wine & Spirits shop in Mill Street in 1910. He sold the shop to Mildenhall Wine Stores in 1920, but continued to manufacture ginger beer and other mineral waters at his factory on the corner of St. Andrew's Street and King Street, until 1926. His premises were knocked down in the early 1970s to make way for Mildenhall's shopping precinct.

25. The International Stores opened in Mill Street in 1909 and continued in business until 1976. This 1931 photograph shows, from the left: Stanley Goodenough of Feltwell, the first hand, Avril Clamp, who came from Walsham-le-Willows but lodged with Mrs. Ellison in St. Andrew's Street, Ivy Thain, the daughter of the licensee of the Maid's Head, apprentice Edward Turner of Barton Mills, apprentice Albert Webb of West Row, apprentice George York of Mildenhall who donated the photograph, Dorothy Ford of West Row, unknown, and Edna Fordham of Mildenhall whose father became manager of Clarke's building firm.

26. No. 4 Mill Street was a tailor's in the hands of the Brown family from at least 1814. Felix Brown added a new shop front in 1888 and his son Charles later advertised that the business had been started in 1772. Charles Stebbing had been a shoemaker at No. 6 for some years when he bought the property in 1878 and in 1901 was advertising that the shop had been going for almost a hundred years. The two men in this photograph of about 1900 are probably Felix Emmanuel Brown and his son Charles. Family marriages brought the shops into common ownership and the businesses continued until 1996 when the shoe shop moved to the High Street. (Courtesy Mr. L. Reeve.)

27. Mr. S.R. Simpson came to Mildenhall in 1868 to take over William Secker's printing works in Mill Street. In 1892 his son Alfred published a History of Mildenhall, which ran to four editions. From 1873 to 1946 the firm produced an annual Almanack & Directory, each containing a retrospect of the previous year, and from 1872 to 1900 published the Mildenhall Monthly Magazine & Advertiser. Bound copies of these works were bequeathed to Mildenhall Museum in 1991 and have been the source of much of the information in this book. Miss Cissie Simpson, granddaughter of the founder, is seen here outside the shop in 1934. This building and the adjacent cottages were knocked down in 1965 to make way for a furniture shop.

28. John L. Saxton was the main author of Simpson's History of Mildenhall and the source of the annual retrospects until his death, aged 84, in 1915. He was born in Boulogne, the son of a runaway marriage between an Irish peer's daughter and her tutor. He trained at Battersea College and then came to Mildenhall to be master of the Bunbury Boys' School for over forty years until retiring in 1893. He was a strict disciplinarian but a thorough teacher and a loyal supporter of many of the local voluntary organisations. His son-in-law, Mr. W. Stockley, was master of the Boys' and Girls' Schools from 1893 to 1921.

29. This photograph, probably from 1896, shows the north side of Mill Street opposite the now Riverside Hotel. The first two houses have changed little over the years but the cottages just before Clinton House were demolished in the 1920s. Clinton House was the home of Dr. Pelham Aldrich in the 1840s and remained a doctor's surgery under his son Arthur and then Dr. Hudson. Dr. Barwell took over in 1908 but in 1933 moved his practice to the Market Place. The house has ever since been a dental surgery. Just beyond the house is a garden, referred to in old deeds as the Burnt Garden, presumably the site of yet another fire.

30. The first house on the left in 1896 was the home of Mr. Frank Parker, an auctioneer, but in the 18th century had been a pub, known once as the Black Horse and later as the King's Head. Next was the photographer's shop run by Mr. L. Wallis, the original source of many of the photographs in this book. Then came a private house, now Marlow's, followed by the watchmaker's shop of the Walker family from the 1870s to 1934; this then moved to St. Andrew's Street. The building at the top of the street was for many years a corn merchant's shop.

PEACE DAY
MILDENHALL
4 July 1919

31. Peace Day was celebrated in Mildenhall on 19th July 1919. Festivities began with a dinner in the town hall for all the servicemen and pensioners living in the town. Then came a procession with bands and decorated floats, sports, tea for all the children and, finally, a firework display. Here we see the parade of children, led by Harry Haylock, coming down Mill Street. The building on the right with the Union Jacks was run by the Misses Hill as the town's first telephone exchange. Next came Ecclestone's drapery shop, advertising in 1889 that it had been established for nearly 200 years. (Courtesy Mr. L. Reeve.)

32. This shows the south side of Mill Street, probably in 1908. The house on the right was known as The Homestead, from 1907 to 1941 the home of the Whiskard family. It was later a vet's surgery and is now Bendall & Sons, solicitors. The present windows are much more in character with the building. The next property remained a private house, at one time for the Whiskards' housekeeper, until the 1950s since when it has been a hairdresser's and, now, Swift Print. On the left was then Oakland House, since restored as a private house by Paul Starling, a former planning officer who did so much to improve Mildenhall in the 1970s.

33. Oakland House, on the left in the last photograph, was in 1700 home to Francis Bugg, a famous local Quaker who wrote some 16 books on his religion. He was also a local trader and issued, as was the custom, trade tokens in lieu of money when coins were scarce. It was already a school when Reverend and Mrs. Burt moved here in 1878. Mrs. Burt continued her Seminary for Young Ladies until 1906. Her daughter then continued a private academy in the church room. Later the house became Arthur Pettit's bakery and then Parker's pet food shop. This 1896 school group was taken in the garden.

34. Flooding is still occasionally a problem in Mildenhall as it was in this 1906 view of Mill Street. The heavy gates to The Homestead have long since been removed as has the massive brick wall that hides what is now the car park of the Riverside Hotel. The Mildenhall Steam Laundry, run by the Parker family, was housed in old stables and outbuildings behind this wall from 1913 until it was destroyed by a fire on Election Night 1959. Parker Bros.' electrical and radio shop was also situated here. The houses on the right remain virtually unchanged.

BRECKLAND SCHOOL MILDENHALL. SUFFOLK.

35. The Riverside Hotel has had a varied history. In the 1800s, before the third storey was added, it was the home of the Isaacson family, solicitors in the town for many years. The building, then known as the Arboretum, was bought by Mrs. Katherine Turner in 1905. She ran a boarding house here until 1912 as well as a laundry, the predecessor of the Steam Laundry. Mr. A. Hall then ran a school here until 1932. It was re-opened as the Breckland School from 1934 to 1940 by Mr. C. Taylor. Later it was a nursing home. This view from the rear is taken from the 1934 school prospectus.

36. There has been a mill in Mildenhall, probably on the present site, at least since Domesday times. Parker Bros. from Barton Mills took over from W.S. Owers in 1897 and, since 1967, have concentrated on animal feeds. Owers had built the 'Hungarian Roller Mills' in 1887 and Parkers extended in 1908. The town's first electricity supply was generated here in 1919, lines being laid to Barton Mills and Worlington in 1932. This 1920s photograph shows the firm's underslung steam tipper lorry in the millyard. Tom Stirges is sitting on the back, Absolom Abrey is standing in the centre and Arthur Bush on the right.

MILDENHALL
GAS WORKS.

37. The Mildenhall Gas Company was established by Mr. G. Madam in 1838 and the gas works erected in 1840. More shares were issued in 1902 and the capital used to build a new gasometer and to extend the gas mains to Kingsway and North Terrace. The town was shocked in November 1912 when Augustine Davenport, the manager, was found drowned in the gas pool. There were many complaints about the street lighting and it was not until 1935 that the lamps were lit on moonlit nights. Electric street lights were installed in 1936 and were much appreciated. The gas works closed in 1958 and the buildings were demolished in the 1970s.

38. This peaceful view of boating on the Lark was taken in 1896. Note the attractive old bridge, demolished and rebuilt in 1985, and the mill in the background. Life was not always so peaceful here for the Cambridge Chronicle of 12th December 1795 records that boats had been sent here from Cambridge the previous Saturday to collect a load of corn. A number of local labourers, led by a man called Docking, opened the sluice gates so that the boats were stranded and then stole a quantity of wheat and barley. Five ringleaders were arrested and sent for trial. This was at a time of great unrest due to low wages and the high price of flour and bread.

39. Barges used to bring goods from King's Lynn to Mildenhall and onwards to Bury St. Edmunds but by 1882 the river was silted up and impassable. The Eastern Counties Navigation & Transport Co. began work in 1889 to restore the waterway. The river was open to Mildenhall by 1891 when the price of coal fell locally. Barges were running to Bury by 1894 but the company then went bankrupt and all commercial traffic soon ceased. The promise of passenger launches was never fulfilled and it remained difficult to get to Bury until a motor bus service started in 1920. This photograph shows work on Mildenhall lock in about 1890.

40. Mildenhall has an attractive river and it is perhaps surprising that little has ever been done to exploit it as an amenity. A Gala and Aquatic Fete was held in 1889 but the weather was atrocious and the event was never repeated. A movement in the 1970s to improve the river so that cabin cruisers could get as far as the town met with great opposition. The Lark Angling & Preservation Society, however, has been active since 1898. Pollution has often been a problem and Simpson notes that in 1926 the Society helped to trace an incident caused by chemicals being released into the river by the Bury sugar beet factory.

41. Mildenhall might have been more prosperous had local landowners not opposed the 1840s plan to run the main London to Norwich line through the town. This was soon regretted and great efforts were made to get a rail link. An act was passed in 1875 authorising a light railway from Ely through Mildenhall to Bury. A celebration dinner was held at the Bell but the line was never built. A branch line from Cambridge was eventually opened in 1885 but was never profitable. Passenger traffic ceased in 1962 and goods traffic in 1964, just as Mildenhall's light industrial estate was being established! (Courtesy Mr. L. Reeve.)

42. Simpson records that in 1905 Mr. F. Morley, a tailor, had erected a wooden building with a very fine shop frontage opposite to Maclaren's. He went on to write, 'It is difficult to find any town of the size of Mildenhall that can excel in shop frontage so elaborate and ornamental.' He can only have been referring to the wooden shack on the left! On the right is to be seen the wall of the manor house, now opened up as Manor Road, and then Maclaren's with Pettit's bakery further on. Note the gas lamp. Could the postman walk down the middle of the street today?

43. On the left Morley's wooden shop has now been replaced by the Post Office, built in 1911 by Mr. R. Clarke on part of Mr. Leach's meadow. Local feelings were hurt when in 1926 this was reduced in status to a sub-Post-Office. It remained here until moving in 1939 to North Terrace in the hands of Mr. Ben Barlow. The building was then bought by Mr. S. Morley who ran a milk bar here before handing over to his son as a bakery. Later it became Mildenhall's first supermarket and then Rumbelow's until 1995. The ground floor has been changed beyond recognition but the upper storey remains unaltered.

44. Duncan Maclaren moved from the Market Place in 1895 to take over the first property on the right in this 1908 view of the High Street. He enlarged the premises in 1902, adding a new shop front and removing all traces of the old Crown Inn, described by Simpson as 'certainly a dismal hostelry'. The Crown had previously been known as the Ram but closed in 1890, becoming then the Conservative Club for five years. The outfitter's shop was continued by the family until 1974 and the site is still known to all locals as Maclaren's, even though it is now, in part, a take-away food shop.

45. The Pettit family had a bakery in the High Street from the 1880s, having earlier been on the corner of the Market Place. William Pettit died in 1890 and his son took over the business, advertising in 1905 that the firm had been established for 119 years. Mrs. Pettit sold the shop in 1928 to Mr. E.A. Hagger whose family ran it as a bakery until 1985. The property has changed little over the years except that the house to the right, now a separate shop, was modernised in the 1950s to serve as a tea room to the bakery. One of the ladies in this 1928 photograph was a Miss Pettit.

46. A Mr. Pope had a book and stationery shop in the High Street, opposite the Market Place, in the 1850s. His successor, Charles Rampling, handed over to William Gale in 1858 to be followed by Charles Palmer by 1865 and Henry Burt in 1898. The shop acted as Mildenhall's Post Office for 25 years until this was moved to Mill Street in 1895 with Charles Palmer as postmaster. Mr. Palmer had also acted as Emigration Agent for the district. Note the Mildenhall Library sign; books could be borrowed for a small fee long before public libraries existed. This photograph shows Mr. Burt outside his shop in 1905.

47. Henry Burt demolished the old building in 1905 and is seen here standing proudly outside his new shop later that year. Mr. Burt lived at Oakland House in Mill Street where his wife ran a private girls' school. He had been the pastor of Mildenhall Baptist Chapel for 25 years but retired in 1899, continuing in business as a stationer until 1920 when Mr. Remmington moved his Cash Boot Stores here from the Market Place. This was then the Eastern Electricity showroom until 1996; the shopfront has been greatly altered but the upper storey remains unchanged.

48. This 1910 postcard of the parish church shows both railings and trees. The railings were removed during the Second World War and the trees, sadly, had to be cut down in 1996. Earlier engravings show that, until the 1851 restoration, the chancel had a low flat roof that left the top of the east window exposed to the elements. The ruin on the left was once a charnel chapel, founded by Ralph de Walsham who, with Simon Domynyk the then vicar of Mildenhall, was involved with the mob that murdered the prior of Bury St. Edmund's Abbey on Mildenhall Heath during the Peasants' Uprising of 1381.

49. The general impression of the interior of the church in 1896 is that of lightness. The present screen between the nave and the chancel, a memorial to Archdeacon Livingstone, was added in 1903. Old prints show high box pews, numbered and rented to individual members of the congregation. These were removed during the 1851 restoration. The pews seen here were in turn removed in 1959 when Mr. H. Munro Cautley, diocesan architect and author of Suffolk Churches, commissioned the present set, with beautifully carved ends, in memory of his wife. The font was moved from its old position and mounted on steps in 1909.

50. The church tower at nearby Isleham collapsed in 1861 and it was then felt that the cracks which had long been evident in Mildenhall's tower should be taken more seriously. Scaffolding was erected in 1864 and the tower resurfaced. The small turret was added at the same time. Lightning struck in 1880, piercing a hole in the wall and scorching the bell frames; a conductor was hastily ordered. The house on the left remains although the ground floor has long since been converted into two shops; the doorway and upper windows are unchanged. To the right is the old Tiger's Head. It is not yet known when this was rebuilt.

51. This picture shows the heavy cast iron gates and twisted gateposts that were removed from the North Porch during the Second World War. Wrought iron gates of a lighter design were added in 1969 in memory of Trevor Hagger. The subject is Harry Haylock who was the church's faithful organ blower for over fifty years. He lived with his unmarried sister, a dressmaker, in a cottage next to Simpson's in Mill Street and died in 1930, aged 76. His youthful appearance here suggests a date around 1890.

52. It is not known when or why this delightful, early photograph of a coach in the High Street was taken. The name on the front, 'Perseverance' may help to solve the mystery. True stage coaches must have made use of the Cock Inn until the early 1800s but later they stopped at the Bull in Barton Mills. In the 1870s, five different local carriers would take passengers as well as goods to Bury, each operating on one or two days a week. There were also daily services to Kennett and Mildenhall Road (Shippea Hill) stations, but they would not have had coaches such as this.

53. The Elizabethan manor house was sold at the final auction of the Bunbury estate in 1933 and demolished in 1934 to make way for building plots. This 1898 view shows what a sad loss this was to the town. At this time, 1897 until 1903, it was leased to the Society of the Sacred Mission as a training college for missionaries. The young priests did much to raise the standard of football in the town and were greatly missed when they moved to Newark. One of the conditions of the lease had been that Sir Henry Bunbury's girls' school should continue to operate in the great hall of the manor house.

West Street, Mildenhall.

83736

54. West Street was renamed Queensway in 1953. This view from the early 1900s shows the Queen's Arms, little changed, on the right. The Gardener's Arms was opposite with the White Swan further back. Westway Cottages, in the distance on the left, were, in the 1830s, a silk manufactory run by Grant, Baylis & Co. Just round the corner into Wamil Way stood the Mildenhall Iron Foundry. The shop on the corner of Wamil Way continued until recent times. The flint wall and house on the left have long disappeared as has the cottage with dormer windows in the centre left.

55. This picture shows the military funeral party for Pte. Richard Dodd coming down Wamil Way in 1917 and it is the only photograph in the museum collection to show this street. The cottages remain more or less unchanged. Wamil Way was previously known as Bridewell Street as the bridewell, or small local prison, used to be here. It was described in a 1780 report as being only one lower room, 11' by 10', and one upper room, 12' by 8', with no fireplace or sewer. The 1669 rules enjoined the keeper to take all prisoners to church twice on Sundays and also to whip them once a week as well as on arrival and on departure.

FUNERAL
OF P. DODD V.T.C.
AT MILDENHALL
MAY 28TH 1917

56. Dr. William Dunn is seen here with his daughter outside his house, the Limes in West Street. He was in practice in Mildenhall from 1894 to 1904, initially by himself in the Market Place and later with Dr. Ord in West Street. Surprisingly, the town, with a population of only some 3,500 at this time, had four doctors. Dr. Dunn has been the only local G.P. to appear in the News of the World. In 1909, after he had moved to Uppingham, he and a local solicitor were the only beneficiaries in the will of a lady who had stayed at The Hall in Mill Street; the only person to object, somewhat unsportingly, to the will was her estranged husband! (Courtesy Market Cross Surgery.)

57. A West Suffolk police force was first established in 1844 and a division was based in Mildenhall. The police station and court house were built in 1851. This 1896 view shows the gate to the pound where stray animals were kept. The window canopies had gone by 1910 and the railings went during the Second World War. Discipline was poor in the early days and one constable was dismissed for allowing a prostitute to stay in his bedroom and to have the keys of the station. Matters greatly improved under Supt. Reeve who was in charge here from 1883 to 1898. He was followed by Supt. Heigham until 1921 when the old Mildenhall division was disbanded.

58. The Wesleyan chapel in the High Street was built in 1829 on the site of the old Slough Pond. The diversion of this water led to regular flooding, often a foot deep, from Police Station Square down to the corner of the High Street. Mr. Arthur Vale, a newly erected parish councillor, was so enraged when this happened yet again in about 1913 that he paid Jimmy Jinks, a local character whose real name was James Curtis, to pretend to be fishing. He also added a stuffed swan to complete the scene. Postcards of this were sold and the council shamed into action. Drains were laid to the river in 1914, to great local rejoicing. (Courtesy Mr. L. Reeve.)

59. A volunteer fire brigade was formed in Mildenhall in 1889, West Row having its own unit. The first firemen to arrive had to collect the keys from the police station and then rush to borrow Mr. Clarke's horses to pull the engine which was kept just round the corner in North Terrace. The old manual engine failed to cope with the fire at the Bridge Mill in 1921 and a new steam engine was then purchased but it was not until 1936 that a motorised vehicle, the gift of Greene King of Bury, was in use. Standing, from the left, in this 1919 group taken outside the police station, are Police Supt. Heigham, Engineer Walter Clarke, Chief Officer Charles Brown, Lieut. Alex Clarke and P.C. Brown.

60. This picture shows the view along North Terrace from Police Station Square in about 1900. On the left is the old fire engine house. Mr. C.H. Toombs' garage was built behind the wall on the left in 1907. He had moved from Thetford to the Market Place as a hairdresser in 1895, branching out as a cycle agent after two years. In 1903 he moved to Police Station Square before opening his garage where the Lark bicycle was made and sold. On the right the Comet Cinema (demolished in 1996), named after the winner of the 1934 Mildenhall to Australia Air Race, was built in 1935 on part of the old Pound Meadow. The new fire station was built alongside in the early 1950s.

61. The east side of North Terrace had been developed in the early 1800s but this view of about 1900 shows that the opposite side was then untouched. Behind the old barn on the right Mr. J. Miller built a large south-facing villa in 1902. Beyond this Mr. Clark built a house for Mr. Brookfield in 1907. The semi-detached houses between this and the garage were erected by Mr. Vale in about 1908 and are faced with Mildenhall brick. The field behind the wall was not developed until 1961. The tree on the left marks the corner of the site where St. Mary's C. of E. Aided Primary School was built in 1902, originally as separate boys' and girls' schools.

62. The last thatched house in the town, known appropriately as the Thatched House, stood at the corner of King Street and Kingsway until it was demolished in 1970 to make way for new houses. It had been owned by Mrs. Fanny Marshall, the widow of a wealthy London timber merchant, who died in 1924. It then became the home of Mr. Sargeant Jaggard, and later his daughters, until the 1940s. The Auxillary Fire Service had a depot in outbuildings here, with an entrance from Kingsway, during the Second World War.

WAR MEMORIAL MILDENHALL BEFORE

63. It had originally been planned to have just one War Memorial for the men of the whole parish but the hamlets decided to go their separate way and so West Row, Beck Row and Kenny Hill all erected their own monuments in 1919. The High Town Memorial, at the junction of King Street and Kingsway, was then built at a cost of £395, raised by public subscription. It is seen here being dedicated on 24th October 1920. Major E.E. Pearson from Bury St. Edmunds and the Reverend H. Wilkinson performed the ceremony in the presence of a crowd of some 2,000.

64. A cannon was placed by the War Memorial a little later and remained until being removed for the scrap metal campaign during the Second World War. This late 1920s photograph shows the Thatched House with its wall extending round into Kingsway. The men in the group are probably, from the left, Charlie Young, Ted Hurrell, Hugh Youngs and Ted Sparrow.

65. This is the most recent photograph to appear in this book but it is the only one that has been discovered to show Market Street before the creation of the somewhat underused 'amenity' area in the late 1960s. The old terraced cottages, typical of so many in the area and including Mr. Gee's bakery shop, have all been demolished but the buildings at the top of the street remains.

66. This picture shows Mr. E.V. Boyce's butcher's shop, at the corner of Market Street and King Street, decorated for the 1909 flower show. The edge of the present Mildenhall Museum can be seen on the left. Mr. Boyce had been in Cemetery Road from 1895 but moved here in 1899, selling out to his manager, Samuel Turner, in 1915. Samuel Turner's son Ray continued the butcher's shop until 1987 since when Bonnett's have converted the building to a complex of small shops and offices. David Turner, Samuel's grandson, opened the Mildenhall Freezer Centre in Kingsway in 1970 on the site of the family's old slaughter house.

KINGSWAY MILDENHALL 4

67. Kingsway presented a very rural appearance when this view was taken, soon after the trees had been planted to commemorate Edward VII's coronation in 1902. There was very little development along here until building plots were made available in 1932. Closer to town Mr. A.H. Baker built his ironmonger's shop, now a grocer's, in 1902 and Horstead Bros. built the first semi-detached houses in 1907. Kingsway had originally been known as the Neatway but later came to be called Kiln Street and then Cemetery Road when the graveyard, in the disused lime pits, was opened in 1869.

68. Mildenhall once had a cottage hospital in Kingsway. This was founded in 1868, largely at the instigation of Dr. F.H. Harris, a local G.P., and was one of the first of its kind in the country. Annual reports were published and show an astonishing range of work being undertaken. Accident victims were treated, with amputations if necessary, tonsils were removed and there was even surgery for cancerous breasts. This photograph, probably from the 1890s, shows the doctors on the left in top hats and the nurses segregated on the right. It seems unkind that the patient with a crooked leg had been given a crooked walking stick.

GROUP AT COTTAGE HOSPITAL BAZAAR
JULY 1st 1909.

69. The central figure in the 1909 Cottage Hospital Bazaar group must be Miss F.M. Turner who was matron from 1906, dying in post after a short illness in 1923. Were so many nurses needed to staff just eight beds? Fund raising events were held regularly but the hospital was always short of money and eventually closed in 1933, unable to afford to modernise sufficiently to compete with the improving facilities at the hospitals in Bury St. Edmunds and Cambridge. The remaining funds were used to establish the Mildenhall, Barton Mills & District Nursing Association that then provided a district nursing service.

70. Sir Thomas Hanmer gave a building in the corner of the churchyard in the 1700s for use as the parish workhouse but this became inadequate when Mildenhall, in 1834, became responsible for a Poor Law Union of thirteen parishes. Eventually in 1895, after years of dispute, a new workhouse was built in Kingsway at a cost of £11,000. The building was commandeered by the army during the First World War and the few inmates of what was by then really an old people's home, were moved to White Lodge, now the Community Hospital in Newmarket. The workhouse proved difficult to sell and went for only £2,550 in 1924. Most of the building was then demolished for scrap but the central part survived until the new police station was built here in 1970.

71. The Mildenhall Board of Guardians had been formed in 1834, to administer the workhouse and outdoor poor relief, but had lost all its powers to national government by 1930 when this final group photograph was taken. Standing, from the left, are: Mr. R. Hitchman, Deputy Clerk, Mr. A. Pearmain, Relieving Officer, Mr. W. Godfery, Sanitary Inspector, Mr. A. Neve, Mrs. M. Bowring, Maj. J. Bowring, Mrs. F. Chandler, Dr. P. Barwell, Medical Officer, Dr. M. O'Leary, Medical Officer, Mrs. F. Lord, the Reverend H. Heap, Mr. G. Peeling, Dr. H. Glasier, Medical Officer, Mr. J. Brown and Mr. A. Llewellyn, Clerk to the R.D.C. Sitting are: the Reverend W. Chandler, Mr. G. Goodwin, the Reverend E. Cockell, Mr. O. Read, Chairman, Mr. J. Dow, Vice-Chairman, Mr. R. Bilsland and the Reverend A. Ard.

The Brick Kilns
Mildenhall

72. The manager's bungalow still stands at the end of Brick Kiln Road but the kilns behind, long disused, were finally demolished to make way for College Heath Road in the 1960s. The brickyard was owned from the 1870s by Robert Goodrich of Providence House in West Street with Robert Vale as manager. Mrs. Goodrich carried on the business after her husband died in 1886 but the industry seems to have ceased just before the First World War. The row of houses just beyond the garage in North Terrace, built in about 1908, is faced with Mildenhall brick. This 1909 postcard was hand painted by Ethel Vale.

73. The town's first football club was formed in September 1879 with the Reverend F.B. Champion as secretary. The game, after some early ups and downs, has been firmly established here ever since. Many team photographs have been preserved but, frustratingly, few have names recorded. This exception shows the Thursday XI of 1913-1914. Standing, from the left, are: E. Cook (linesman), L. Rolfe, J. Mansfield and H.S. Clarke (Vice-Captain); kneeling are: M. Williams, F. Williams (Captain) and J. Leach; sitting are: L. Bryon, A. Mutton. A.W. Neve (Secretary), A.B. Barnes and W. Lindsay. This team played on Mildenhall's early closing day.(Courtesy Mr. L. Reeve.)

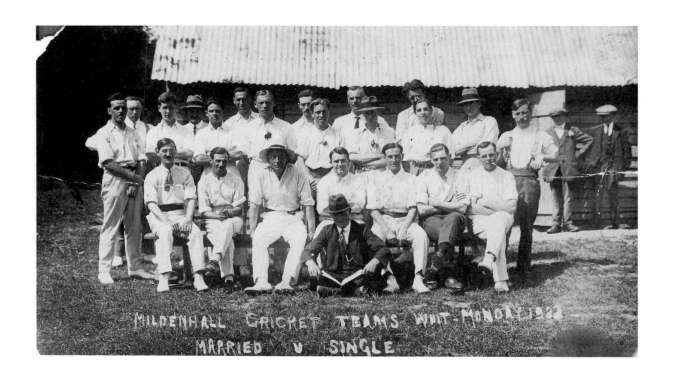

MILDENHALL CRICKET TEAMS WHIT-MONDAY 1922
MARRIED V SINGLE

74. Mildenhall Cricket Club celebrated its centenary in 1976 but Simpson in fact records in 1876 that the club had then been restarted after a lapse of several years. Sir Henry C.J. Bunbury succeeded his father in 1885 and was president until his death in 1931. It was not until after the Second World War that the club shed its upper-class image and welcomed all to its ranks. The club played on a variety of pitches before moving to the top of St. Andrew's Street in 1901 and then to its present site in 1972. This photograph shows the married v. single match teams on Whit Monday 1922. (Courtesy Mrs. S. Grinling.)

"OFFICERS" OF THE MILDENHALL "CHURCH LADS' BRIGADE 1908.

75. The Church Lads' Brigade held its first drill on Shrove Tuesday 1899 and is still, as the Boys' Brigade, going strong. Mr. H.E. Wall, a lay reader from Kenny Hill, was captain until 1901. The scouting movement started in 1908 and Mildenhall's troop was officially registered in 1919, although it had been active at least from 1916. Maurice Williams was scoutmaster from 1921 to 1970 and laid the foundation of the new scout hut in 1980. No early photographs of the scouts have yet been discovered but this shows the officers of the Church Lads' Brigade in 1908.

76. We end with a general view of the town centre, taken from the church tower in about 1910. The group of buildings at the top of the Market Square was demolished in 1960 to make way for the new shopping precinct but the L-shaped flint cottages at the rear of the group remain and are now the Mildenhall Museum, where the originals of most of the photographs in this book can be seen. The façade of the house on the corner of Market Street has been preserved but the rest of the building is modern. The open fields beyond the town are now covered by housing estates but, otherwise, little has changed.